JAN   2003

The Wonder of
ELEPHANTS

For Aunt Jean
 — Anthony D. Fredericks

Please visit our web site at: www.garethstevens.com
For a free color catalog describing Gareth Stevens Publishing's list of high-quality books
and multimedia programs, call 1-800-542-2595 (USA) or 1-800-461-9120 (Canada).
Gareth Stevens Publishing's Fax: (414) 332-3567.

Library of Congress Cataloging-in-Publication Data

Lantier, Patricia.
    The wonder of elephants / by Patricia Lantier and Anthony D. Fredericks;
  illustrated by John F. McGee.
       p. cm. — (Animal wonders)
  Includes index.
  "Based on . . . Elephant magic for kids . . . by Anthony D. Fredericks"—T.p. verso.
  ISBN 0-8368-2764-3 (lib. bdg.)
  1. Elephants—Juvenile literature. [1. Elephants.] I. Fredericks, Anthony D.
  II. McGee, John F., ill. III. Title. IV. Series.
  QL737.P98L267   2001
  599.67—dc21   00-051629

First published in North America in 2001 by
Gareth Stevens Publishing
A World Almanac Education Group Company
330 West Olive Street, Suite 100
Milwaukee, WI 53212 USA

This edition is based on the book *Elephants for Kids,* text © 1999 by Anthony D. Fredericks, with
illustrations by John F. McGee, first published in the United States in 1999 by NorthWord Press,
(Creative Publishing international, Inc.), Minnetonka, MN, and published as *Elephant Magic for
Kids* in a library edition by Gareth Stevens, Inc., in 2000. Additional end matter © 2001 by
Gareth Stevens, Inc.

Photographs © 1998: Mark J. Thomas/Dembinsky Photo Associates: Cover, 16-17; Joe
McDonald/Tom Stack & Associates: 23, 44-45; Art Wolfe: 4-5, 14, 36-37; Tom & Pat Leeson:
10-11, 20, 24, 31, 34-35, 38, 40, 43, 47; Stan Osolinski/Dembinsky Photo Associates: 13, 32;
W. Perry Conway/Tom Stack & Associates: 18-19; John Shaw/Tom Stack & Associates: 26-27;
Roy Toft/Tom Stack & Associates: 28-29.

Printed in the United States of America

1 2 3 4 5 6 7 8 9 05 04 03 02 01

The Wonder of
ELEPHANTS

by Patricia Lantier and Anthony D. Fredericks
Illustrations by John F. McGee

Gareth Stevens Publishing
A WORLD ALMANAC EDUCATION GROUP COMPANY

Elephants are huge animals with flexible trunks and long, white tusks. They also have flapping ears and thin tails that can grow to more than 5 feet (1.5 meters) long.

Elephants travel in groups called herds.

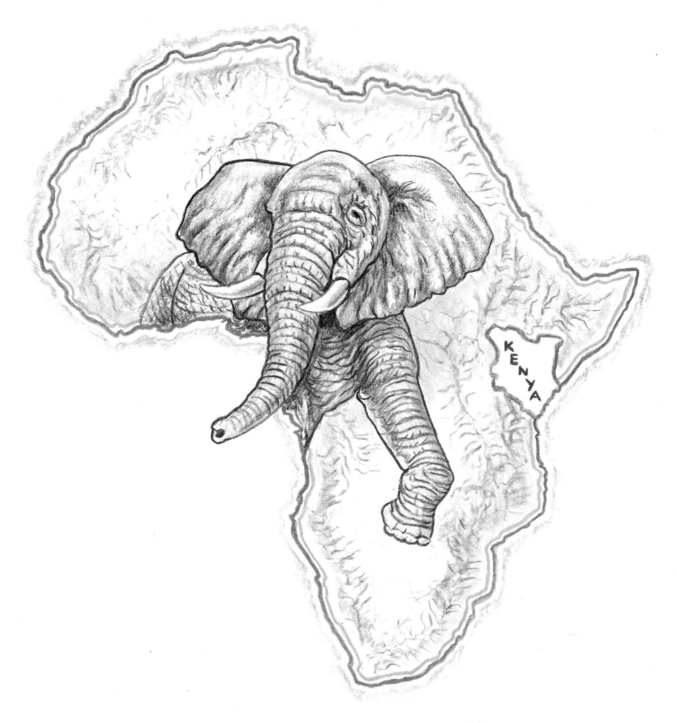

KENYA

A male elephant is called a bull. A female elephant is called a cow. A baby elephant is called a calf.

There are two species, or kinds, of elephants — African elephants and Asian elephants. African elephants live in central and southern Africa, in countries such as Kenya.

An African bull elephant can weigh up to 15,000 pounds (6,800 kilograms) — as much as a school bus!

Adult African elephants can stand up to 13 feet (4 m) high. They are the world's largest land mammals.

African elephant (on next page)

Asian elephants live in India and some countries in Southeast Asia. These elephants are smaller than their African relatives. An Asian bull elephant can weigh up to 12,000 pounds (5,443 kg) and stands about 10 feet (3 m) tall. Asian elephants also have smaller ears than African elephants.

Asian elephants

Although elephants are very large, they are able to run short distances as fast as a galloping horse.

Elephants walk on tiptoes!
They have thick pads
behind their toes to help
hold their weight.

Adult bulls live alone or with other bulls. Cows and calves live in their own herds, led by an older female called a matriarch.

African elephants (also on next page)

Elephants are intelligent animals, and they have good memories. The matriarch may have the best memory in the herd because she has lived longer and traveled more than any of the other elephants. She remembers where to find the best food and water, as well as which direction to travel.

Elephants use their long, flexible trunks to drink water or to spray themselves in hot weather. Sometimes elephants even greet each other by wrapping their trunks together!

Asian elephant

An elephant can hold up to 3 gallons (11 liters) of water in its trunk at one time. To take a drink, it squirts the water into its mouth.

Elephants also use their trunks to smell and to pick up objects — some as tiny as berries. Their trunks can reach tall branches, too, even higher than a giraffe can reach!

Elephants have two tusks that grow from their upper jaws. These tusks are very long teeth, called incisors. Tusks are made of ivory.

Both male and female African elephants have tusks. Many Asian elephants do not have tusks, or their tusks are too small to see.

Asian elephant

Elephants use their tusks to dig for food and water and as weapons to protect their territories. The world's heaviest African elephant tusk weighs 259 pounds (117 kg). The longest tusk ever measured is 11.5 feet (3.5 m).

African elephant

Elephants use
their large, floppy
ears to keep cool.
In hot weather,
they flap their
ears to create
a nice breeze.

Elephants can "talk" with their ears, too. A herd's matriarch sticks her ears out to warn the other elephants of danger.

Elephants also use low, rumbling sounds to talk to each other. They can hear these sounds up to 6 miles (10 kilometers) away.

If an elephant is upset,
it may raise its trunk
high into the air and
make a loud sound
like a trumpet.

A full-grown elephant
needs to eat up to 400
pounds (180 kg) of plants
every day.

Adult elephants can drink 3 gallons (11 l) of water at a time and up to 24 gallons (90 l) of water in one day. That's like drinking 384 glasses of water a day!

To keep cool, elephants must spray themselves with water or take mud baths. The moisture from the showers or mud baths gets trapped in their wrinkly skin. The trapped moisture keeps an elephant cool for a longer time than if the animal had smooth skin.

Elephant cows have one calf about every four years. A mother elephant carries the calf inside her for almost two years. Calves can weigh up to 350 pounds (160 kg) at birth.

Elephants are gentle and brave animals that need lots of room to survive in their natural habitats.

Today, many people around the world are working hard to protect elephants and their habitats. There are special areas in Africa and Asia where elephants can live safely in the wild.

Glossary

flexible — able to move and bend easily in different directions

habitats — the places where animals and plants live in nature

herd — a group of animals that travels together

incisors — special cutting teeth often found in mammals

intelligent — able to learn

ivory — a hard, cream-colored material that forms the tusks of elephants

mammals — warm-blooded animals that feed their young with mother's milk

matriarch — a female elephant, usually the oldest, that leads the herd

species — a group of animals or plants with similar characteristics

Index